# The CALEDONIAN CANAL
## Lochs, Locks and Pleasure Steamers

*by*
Guthrie Hutton

*Gondolier* approaching Banavie.

© Guthrie Hutton 1998
First Published in the United Kingdom, 1998
by Stenlake Publishing, Ochiltree Sawmill,
The Lade, Ochiltree, Ayrshire KA18 2NX
Tel/Fax 01290 423114

ISBN 1 84033 033 3

The steamer *Glengarry* alongside Muirtown Wharf.

# Canal Through The Mountains

The idea of a canal from sea to sea linking the lochs of the Great Glen had been around for a long time. Even while the Jacobite clans of the Glen were joining successive rebellions against the Hanoverian monarchy, surveyors, as if in another time zone, were selecting routes and drawing plans. But after their crushing defeat at the Battle of Culloden the Jacobite clans were harried mercilessly and their way of life destroyed. A steady stream of people began to leave the glens. The exodus went on for fifty years before an anxious Government sought to stem the tide of emigration by commissioning public works in the Highlands. The biggest project was the Caledonian Canal.

The great Scottish engineer Thomas Telford was engaged to prepare plans. He surveyed the route and presented designs for a twenty feet deep canal, with locks large enough for naval frigates and Baltic traders. It was a highly ambitious scheme and on a scale that had never been attempted before. Furthermore, it was to be built with a largely unskilled local labour force, led by only a few experienced engineers and craftsmen. Nevertheless the Government accepted the plans and work started in 1803.

Almost at once the vagaries of Highland weather and the enormity of the task overwhelmed Telford's initial estimates. The project soared past its financial and completion targets. It was expected to take seven years and £350,000 to build, but, when it opened in 1822 it had taken nineteen years and £840,000, and it was only fourteen feet deep

While critics grumbled about the constant drain on public finances the substandard canal stuttered along until 1844, when its supporters persuaded the authorities to close it and have it brought up to the standard proposed by Telford. When it reopened in 1847 it was substantially the canal that can be seen today, although some early construction defects that went undetected in the 1840s have continued to force more closures in recent years. Despite this, it remains a remarkable achievement and one of the crowning glories of Scottish civil engineering history.

The Caledonian Canal has also become one of Scotland's great attractions, as tourists from Victorian times to the present day have enjoyed sailing through its glorious scenery. Since the 1930s there has been the added prospect of seeing another of our great tourist attractions, the Loch Ness Monster.

Guthrie Hutton, 1998.

A Banff registered fishing boat slips through Tomnahurich Bridge.

ON THE BANKS OF THE
CALEDONIAN CANAL.

1364

Muirtown Basin covered twenty acres and was intended to provide Inverness with a non-tidal second harbour, but by the time the canal was opened many coasting vessels were too big for the locks. As boats would also have had to sail past the harbour entrance to reach the canal, it seems unlikely that the basin would ever have achieved its potential. Nevertheless the excavation of such an extensive inland harbour was a remarkable achievement and its sheer size is apparent in this picture of the *Gatelifter* and maintenance barges just above Clachnaharry Works Lock. Over the years there have been three *Gatelifter* barges designed and built for the task of transporting and fitting the huge lock gates.

Muirtown was transformed into a hive of activity during the First World War when it was used as an American Naval base. At other times the fishing fleet crowded into the basin, but here, just below Muirtown Bridge, only two boats and a small steam coaster lie alongside. The basin also failed to attract manufacturing industry and so instead of works and warehousing the main commercial activity on the waterfront was making whisky. One of two distilleries that operated in the area can be seen behind the boats to the right of the Muirtown Hotel. Over the years the hotel provided lodgings for canal men, ship owners and passengers alike.

The distilleries are prominent on the right here as a veritable shoal of fishing boats makes its way up the Muirtown Locks. At different times of the year that most fished of fish, the herring, migrated from one side of the country to the other. The east coast fishing fleet went after them, but instead of risking the dangerous Pentland Firth the boats used the canal. In the late twentieth century the canal has begun to show signs of age and, despite being better built than some of the more remote locks, Muirtown has had its difficulties. In 1976, only three years after a major overhaul, a pair of gates collapsed swamping a cabin cruiser and much of the surrounding area.

MUIRTON, CALEDONIAN CANAL, INVERNESS.

*Sept. 19-99-Here we are at the most Northern point of our wanderings. Have had rain with intervals of pleasant weather the past week. Start for Oban at 6 30 to-morrow morning, where I expect more rain. I hope to persuade Y to go by Steamer with me instead of cycling. Went to Cathedral Service yesterday afternoon & ...*

There are four staircase locks in the Muirtown flight, seen here being climbed by a little paddle steamer. This early picture postcard was sent to Boston in 1899, at a time when such cards were a rarity; one showing the canal says much about its value to the local tourist trade. The message too says much about the late nineteenth century tourist; undaunted by an early start, expecting bad weather and fortified by a cathedral service, the writer's only concern seems to be to persuade their companion to travel to Oban by steamer instead of going by bicycle. Such intrepid explorers make today's package tourists look like wimps!

The departure point for our Oban-bound tourist, and indeed any passenger leaving Inverness on one of the paddle steamers, was the wharf at the top of Muirtown Locks. Here the *Gondolier* has just arrived and sparked off an excited melee of holidaymakers jostling to get themselves and their luggage onto one of the horse drawn omnibuses. Big hotels sent their own buses to meet the steamers. The Palace, the hotel whose bus is in the foreground, was closest to the wharf, which was no doubt an attraction to those tourists who wanted an extra five minutes in bed before catching the early boat!

*Caledonian Canal, Inverness.*  664

One of the improvements made to the canal in the 1840s was the creation of a turning point for the steamers at Burnfoot. The canal builders had probably expected the harbour facilities of Muirtown Basin to attract boats down the locks, but the steamers could not afford the time so they stopped at the top. This appears to have caused a rethink because Burnfoot, not Muirtown, became the maintenance and winter base for the steamers. The small yacht lying alongside the Burnfoot base with *Gairlochy* is perhaps a sign of things to come, because the old steamer base is now used by Caledonian Cruisers, the oldest fleet operator of hire cruisers on the canal.

Two small paddler steamers, *Glengarry* and *Lochness*, provided a year round link for passengers, cargo and the Royal Mail between Inverness and the communities around Loch Ness. Roads were poor and the railway from Spean Bridge only reached Fort Augustus, so the canal was the transport lifeline. This picture of *Glengarry* was taken near the distinctive hill of Tomnahurich. It is a feature left over from the ice ages when sub-glacial meltwater flowed out of the Great Glen leaving behind heaped deposits of sand and gravel. Other glacial mounds or terraces can be seen from the canal at Torvean and Dochgarroch.

Although the Great Glen was formed some 380 million years ago it is still seismically active. Buildings in Inverness were damaged by an earth tremor in 1816 and a long crack appeared in the towpath of the canal near Dochgarroch after another quake in 1901. Dochgarroch Lock, at the end of the canal channel from Inverness, is a regulating lock designed to protect the canal and Inverness from fluctuating water levels on Loch Ness. The rise or fall of a vessel going through it can, therefore, be disappointingly small if it is someone's first experience of a lock. Here *Gondolier* is working through the lock on her way to Inverness.

*S. S. Loch Ness on Loch Ness.*

Arch<sup>d</sup> Macintyre, Fort William

*Caledonian Canal.*

Although the number of lochs linked together to form the canal is usually quoted as three, there are actually four; the fourth is Loch Dochfour. It is at the northern end of Loch Ness and was originally a shallow body of water, in effect a widening of the River Ness, which had to be dredged to the depth of the canal. A towing path, seen here on the right, was laid through it on a causeway that later became part of the main A82 road. The boat is *Lochness* and the publisher of this old postcard clearly couldn't resist the delicious coincidence of a boat sailing on a loch of the same name and was not going to let a small detail – like it being the wrong loch – get in the way of a good caption!

THE BEACH AT LOCHEND, LOCH NESS

D 244

Lochend beach at the northern end of Loch Ness was a popular place for Invernesians to cool down on sunny days. The temperature of the loch water averages a chilly 6°, hardly varying between summer and winter, and the absence of bathers here suggests that something hotter than the average Scottish summer would be needed to tempt these folk into the loch for a swim. Lochend is also a popular starting point to go fishing on the loch from a rowing boat. The white building in the distance on the right is the Bona lighthouse. It marked the entrance to the canal from Loch Ness and was unusual in that it was manned, and some miles from the sea.

TEMPLE PIER, LOCH NESS, GLEN URQUHART.     200035 J.V.

Temple Pier, seen here with *Gondolier* and a sailing vessel alongside, was the pier for Drumnadrochit, a village that has found a new role as a centre for monster hunters since the halcyon days of the paddle steamers. The first sighting of a Loch Ness Monster was in AD 565 when Saint Columba apparently saw a water horse in the River Ness. After that, despite many thousands of steamer passengers gazing wistfully across the loch, it all went quiet until 1933 when the *Inverness Courier* reported a sighting by a Fort Augustus water bailiff. Since then Nessie has 'appeared' many times and attracted many tourists to Loch Ness and Drumnadrochit.

LOCH NESS AT DRUMNADROCHIT 516

With Drumnadrochit set back from the shallow Urquhart Bay, Temple Pier was in deep water over a mile from the village. In approaching it from the south the steamers passed close in to Castle Urquhart and then swept across the bay before turning back towards Loch Ness and coming alongside. *Gairlochy* is seen here near the pier with Castle Urquhart on the distant promontory. The castle was a focus for unrest for centuries until 1692 when its garrison blew up some of the buildings to render it useless to their Jacobite enemies. Time, neglect, robbery and a February storm in 1715 completed the castle's ruin.

Foyers, on the south side of the loch, was a favourite stop for the steamer passengers who came to marvel at the raw power of the 90 foot falls on the River Foyers. That power was harnessed in 1896 when water from the river was diverted to generate the first hydro-electricity in Britain. It was used by an aluminium works at Lower Foyers which continued in operation up to the 1960s. It made the canal into an industrial waterway with ships, like this coaster, moving materials and supplies to and from the pier. The pioneering generating plant has now been replaced by a modern hydro-electric station that uses surplus power to pump water up to its reservoir, from where it falls back down to generate more electricity.

93147.    *The Pier, Invermoriston.*    J.V.

Further south, on the loch's northern shore, is Invermoriston, another of the communities served by the steamers. The pier was about a mile from the village and is seen here with the steamer *Lochness* approaching from the shallow bay at the mouth of the River Moriston. She was built in 1853 as the *Lochgoil* and after service on the Clyde went to Ireland where she worked as the *Lough Foyle*. She returned to the Clyde in 1877 and was bought eight years later by David MacBrayne's. They shortened her, added a new bow and saloon accommodation, changed her name to *Lochness* and sent her to work on the canal. She continued in service until she was scrapped in 1912.

Loch Ness, at Fort Augustus.

992

The canal and River Oich enter Loch Ness at Fort Augustus side by side. They are seperated by a narrow strip of land, and Inveroich Pier, where the Loch Ness steamers terminated their run down the loch, was on the canal side of it. The steamer sitting alongside here is the *Glengarry*. Originally known as *Edinburgh Castle II*, she spent two years on the Clyde before starting service on the canal in 1846. Thirty years later she emerged from an extensive refit, longer and with her new name. When she was withdrawn in 1927, at the grand old age of 83, she was reckoned to be the oldest steamer in the world.

1771. S.S. "Gondolier" entering Loch Ness, Fort Augustus.

*Glengarry* is seen here in the distance at Inveroich Pier as *Gondolier* heads for Loch Ness on the last leg of a journey that for many of her passengers would have begun on the Clyde. The route from Glasgow, through the Crinan Canal, up the West Coast and on through the Caledonian Canal was known as the 'Royal Route' after Queen Victoria and Prince Albert travelled along it at various times. In 1873 Queen Victoria sailed from Banavie to Dochgarroch on the *Gondolier*, 26 years to the day after Albert had first travelled through the canal. The Queen apparently found the hold-ups in the locks unamusing and would no doubt have approved of *Gondolier's* turn of speed here.

The lock flights on the Caledonian Canal were built as continuous staircases with no intermediate pounds for boats to pass each other. This meant that a large boat arriving at the locks while they were in use by an equally large boat going in the opposite direction had to wait until it had cleared them – and there are five locks at Fort Augustus! Fishing boat crews found the delays particularly frustrating because when they were not fishing, they were not earning. These steam drifters are being held up below the Fort Augustus locks while another boat completes its descent to the Loch Ness level.

The drifters on the facing page were waiting for a puffer, seen here heading out of the lock past the crowd of fishing boats. Puffers developed from steam-driven Forth and Clyde Canal lighters to become the ubiquitous little steam coasters made famous in the stories of Para Handy and the *Vital Spark*. The name comes from the puffing sound made by the exhausts of the early lighters and, although more sophisticated later vessels like this one photographed in the 1920s, didn't 'puff', the name stuck. Puffers are not usually associated with the Caledonian Canal, but became a familiar sight on it after the Foyers plant opened.

THE LOCKS OF THE CALEDONIAN CANAL AT FORT AUGUSTUS.

After the Jacobite uprisings of 1715 and 1719 the Government sought to pacify the clans of the Great Glen by building three forts, one at each end – Fort William and Fort George – and one in the middle at the strategically important little village of Killichuimen. It was called Fort Augustus and gave its name to the village too. The fort was well sited beside Loch Ness on a peninsula formed by the Oich and Tarff Rivers, but with the defeat of the Jacobite uprising of 1745/46, its job was done. A garrison remained until the Crimean War period, but the old fort was demolished in 1876 and the Benedictine Abbey, seen behind the locks here, was built on the site.

CALEDONIAN CANAL, THE LOCKS AT FORT AUGUSTUS. 1358.

This splendid panorama of the village was taken in 1878 soon after the Abbey tower was built and shows how little of the present day village existed at that time. The canal dominates the small community with the paved circles for operating the lock gate capstans clearly visible beside each pair of gates. To the right is the River Oich which was diverted to make way for the canal. Its original course took it in a wide arc in front of the houses on the left and back across to the right foreground where the canal occupies the original river bed. An early version of the Lovat Arms Hotel can be seen at the top of the village on the left.

S.S. GONDOLIER, IN THE LOCKS, FORT AUGUSTUS

Fort Augustus was a long and inconvenient way from Inverness and before the canal was built it was not easy for the engineers to get around the construction sites. The temptation therefore for contractors to skimp on the work must have been great, and the locks were not well built. One collapsed in 1837 and had to be rebuilt; more recently British Waterways have incurred huge expense to stabilise masonry in danger of collapse. The trestle and grouting tools lying on the lock side suggest that constant maintenance of the stonework was needed and has only stopped briefly here to allow *Gondolier* to pass.

The Locks, Fort Augustus.

Most pictures of the canal, like the one opposite, create the impression that the Great Glen is blessed with permanent summer and bathed in perpetual sunshine. It is not, and having struggled up the canal in an inflatable boat into a sleet-laden north-easterly gale, I can vouch for it being occasionally less than sylvan – in May! If you doubt the Glen's ability to slip its mask, this picture of a snowy Fort Augustus should convince you that when the tourists have gone and the steamers are laid up for the winter, a cold and sometimes bleak prospect can face those who trade along the canal.

43157 J.V.

Fort Augustus

Fort Augustus was the only sizeable community along the length of the canal and, give or take the odd half hour or so, was reached about half-way through a steamer trip. The journey took over seven hours and, by the time the steamers reached Fort Augustus the passengers, particularly those from the south, would be itching to get off and stretch their legs. They had forty-five minutes to sample the attractions of the little town while the boat was working through the locks. Some made a dash to look at the monastery, while others preferred a more leisurely inspection of the wares on offer at the lockside shops. They specialised in 'Highland' souvenirs and postcards – like this one.

Entering the Caledonian Canal at Fort Augustus.

The swing bridge that carried the Invergarry and Fort Augustus Railway across the canal to its pier on Loch Ness, is to the right of *Gondolier* entering Fort Augustus top lock. The railway should perhaps never have been built. It was blocked by the Highland Railway Company from going all the way up the Great Glen to Inverness, yet undaunted the line's backers pressed on with an extravagantly engineered line from Spean Bridge to Fort Augustus. It opened in 1903, but after only three years the mile long extension to Loch Ness, including the swing bridge and an expensive viaduct over the River Oich, was closed. The railway was a spectacular failure, hirpling from one crisis to another until it was finally closed in 1946.

*Gondolier*, seen here leaving Fort Augustus for Banavie in 1891, was put on the canal in 1866 by David Hutcheson and Company. Unlike the steamers that subsequently joined her, she was built specially for the canal. The blunt bow and square stern, needed for working through locks, contrasted sharply with the sleek yacht-like appearance of the company's coastal steamers. When the Hutchesons retired from the business their former partner David MacBrayne took the company over, and from 1879 operated it in his own name. It was a name that became synonymous with West Coast and canal steamers, giving rise to the cheeky saying that; 'The Lord owns the world and all it contains, except the West Highlands which belong to MacBrayne's'.

S.S. GONDOLIER LEAVING FORT AUGUSTUS.

Although *Gondolier's* hull was shaped to fit the canal locks it would not have been easy for helmsmen to steer through locks and bridges from a wheel positioned behind the funnel. She operated the Banavie – Inverness run with *Glengarry*, *Gairlochy* and *Glengarry* again up to the late 1920s but through the 1930s worked the route alone. Her saloons were improved in the mid-1930s, but trade dwindled and she was withdrawn at the start of the Second World War. She was taken over by the Admiralty, stripped down to a hulk and towed to the naval base at Scapa Flow. There she was sunk as a defence against submarines after one had breached the harbour defences and sunk the battleship H.M.S. *Royal Oak*.

Kytra Lock was built in a remote and lonely spot and because of its isolation the engineers decided to construct it with locally quarried granite on a natural rock base, rather than bringing stone from Inverness. It is about two and a half miles by canal and private road from Fort Augustus and was an isolated place for lock keepers and their families to live. They were allowed to keep a cow as well as chickens, and grow their own produce. Even today, because the modern road south of Fort Augustus veers away from the canal, the only way to see Kytra Lock is to go by boat or walk along the towpath.

Despite their isolation the lock keepers were kept in touch with the outside world by the passengers and crews of passing vessels like the *Gondolier*. Passengers on steamers heading east used to get off at Kytra and walk to Fort Augustus. It must have felt like an adventure to be left behind by the steamer as it headed for Fort Augustus, although all but the most nervous would have been comforted by the knowledge that they would catch it up again as it slowly descended the locks. It was a lovely, tranquil walk too, because the rocky offside bank between Fort Augustus and Kytra makes the canal look more natural than artificial.

Two miles from Kytra is Cullochy Lock, the top lock on the rise from the east coast. Like Kytra it was built on a rock base with locally quarried granite. The granite was very tough and difficult to work, but was persisted with because the alternative of bringing stone from the east coast was impractical. Some freestone was needed in the construction, but the builders waited until the canal was opened before bringing the heavy load to the unfinished lock by boat. As with so many of the locks, serious construction defects were discovered in the late 1980s and in a major overhaul, the old masonry structure was grouted, sealed, buttressed and cocooned in concrete.

Cullochy is half a mile or so from Loch Oich making it slightly less remote than Kytra. It is reached from the loch-side road crossing this bridge behind *Gondolier*. All but one of the original double leaf cast iron bridges have been replaced by swing bridges. This one, Aberchalder Bridge, was replaced in the 1930s as part of a major scheme to improve the road from Fort William to Inverness. Aberchalder was where Bonnie Prince Charlie mustered his Jacobite army before marching south in 1745. Sixty years later, men from those same Highland clans were cutting the canal past the historic site.

S.S. GAIRLOCHY PASSING S.S. GONDOLIER, LOCH OICH.

Loch Oich forms the canal's summit reach which remarkably in such mountainous country is only 106 feet above sea level. The level of the loch is maintained by a weir at its northern end which the River Oich flows over at the start of its short course to Loch Ness. Loch Oich was quite shallow until its level was fixed and bed dredged; vessels working through the canal have to take care not to stray outside the buoyed channel. Here *Gairlochy* and *Gondolier* chop up the surface of the water as they pass at close quarters. The two steamers operated daily throughout the summer season from either end of the canal and usually passed on the loch.

Precise timing is not easy to guarantee on a canal and on this occasion, for whatever reason, it appears to have gone awry because instead of passing on Loch Oich the steamers have met at Laggan Locks. The picture was taken from *Gondolier* in the top lock; waiting to enter, half hidden behind the man in plus fours, is *Gairlochy*. She has evidently made better time from Inverness than *Gondolier* has from Banavie. The men on the lock gate are opening the paddles to fill the lock. In the background is Laggan Avenue, a private world of mature conifers that binds the soil of the deep canal cutting from Loch Oich.

The Laggan Avenue cutting was a huge undertaking which tested the engineers' ingenuity. So too were the Laggan Locks. They had to be built on soft ground and Telford reduced the scale of construction by damming the outfall of Loch Lochy into the Spean River. This raised the level of the loch by twelve feet which cut down on the number of locks needed at Laggan. Here *Gondolier* is seen entering the bottom of the two locks from Loch Lochy. Beside the lock, on the right, is the little shop that catered for steamer passengers. The steamers took on passengers at all convenient points and the people on the left could be waiting to join the boat, or just watching – a pastime as popular then as it is now.

Before they were converted to work hydraulically, the lock gates were hauled open and shut by sub-surface chains operated by capstans like this one on the bottom lock at Laggan. There were two capstans for each gate, one to open and one to close it and it took seven revolutions of the capstan to complete each operation. Everybody lent a hand; the man on the right of this picture from around 1900 appears to be 'Paddy', a lock side busker who, along with the boy beside him, entertained passengers with Irish music and dance. Behind them all, carved across the lower slopes of the hills, is a very new looking Invergarry and Fort Augustus Railway.

At the southern end of the ten mile long Loch Lochy is Gairlochy (the place, not the steamer!) where there was, like Dochgarroch, originally only one regulating lock. In 1834 it was swamped by flood water when the outfall into the Spean River was blocked by debris during heavy rain. Had the lock failed an unstoppable flood would have descended on Banavie and Corpach. It was a salutary lesson and a second lock was built as a defence against any similar occurrence. This picture shows the new lock with *Gondolier* waiting to be raised to the level of Loch Lochy.

*SS "Gondolier" entering Gairlochy Lock, Caledonian Canal. 8952*

The new lock was built in 1844 while the canal was closed for remedial works. It was separated from the lower lock by a large pound, seen here from the western bank with *Gondolier* approaching the upper lock. Some of her passengers have taken the chance of a short stroll around the pound. Out of picture to the right is a distinctive bow-fronted lock keeper's house. It was erected on site first so that skilled men, building the original lock, could use it as a bunk house. Telford also stayed at the building during his site visits. The same tactic was used to provide accommodation at other remote construction sites although the ordinary navvies had to fend for themselves and made turf huts to shelter in.

The canal steamers did not go all the way down to Corpach, but terminated above the lock flight at Banavie. Passengers continuing their journeys to the south and Glasgow were taken on to Corpach by horse-drawn omnibus. From 1895 they had an alternative when a branch line from the West Highland Railway at Fort William was opened. It ran to a station at the foot of the canal embankment and people had to climb up or down to it from the new pier. The locomotive seen here has shunted waggons up a zig-zag siding to the canal side so that goods could be more easily transferred between train and steamer.

*Gairlochy*, seen here above the Banavie locks, had worked on the Clyde for over thirty years when David MacBrayne bought her for service on the canal. She was shortened by about 30 feet, her bow and stern were rebuilt and a saloon was added in a re-fit that brought her up to the standard of a MacBrayne boat. She started operating on the Banavie to Inverness run in 1895. Normally she and *Gondolier* were laid up at Burnfoot for the winter, but on Christmas Eve 1919, while working the Loch Ness service, she caught fire at Fort Augustus and was burned to the waterline. The hulk can still be seen behind Inveroich Pier.

The eight Banavie Locks, more popularly known as Neptune's Staircase, extend for over a quarter of a mile and make up what is arguably the most impressive feature on the whole canal. The old manually operated wheel mechanism for operating the gate paddles can be seen in this 1870s picture. Both the paddles and the old gate opening capstans have been replaced by hydraulics and the entire operation to open and close the gates is worked by a single lock-keeper from a lock-side control panel. The bow fronted lock-keeper's house can be seen, half-hidden by trees, to the right of where a mast protrudes from a lock. Banavie Hotel is on the extreme right.

"NEPTUNE'S STAIRCASE", CALEDONIAN CANAL, FORT WILLIAM. 223258.

Behind the steam drifter making her ascent of Neptune's Staircase are two swing bridges. One, which is still open, was erected in the 1930s to take a realigned Loch Eil-side road across the canal. It superseded a double leaf swing bridge which crossed the third lock up the flight. The lattice girder swing bridge behind the fishing boat carries the West Highland Railway extension to Mallaig across the canal. Opened in 1901, it is one of the finest scenic railways in Europe. It is still used by steam hauled excursion trains, although diesels have to take over when track-side vegetation is dry and likely to be ignited by flying sparks.

Neptune's Staircase, Banavie.

This ship, in the bottom lock of Neptune's Staircase, is David MacBrayne's *Cavalier*, a 360 ton coaster that worked a weekly round trip between Glasgow and Inverness. She was built in 1883 and is believed to have been the first ship sailing from the Clyde to be lit by electricity. She had a stocky hull and square stern, a shape dictated by the canal locks, but she was also a good sea boat, which was no doubt appreciated by her passengers while in the notoriously rough seas off the Mull of Kintyre. Although she carried passengers she was primarily a cargo vessel, but with trade dwindling she was taken off in 1919.

91979 J V

With the name partially obscured it is difficult to be positive about the identity of this boat below Neptune's Staircase, but with her traditional 'puffer-like' lines betraying Forth and Clyde Canal origins, she could be the *Starfinch*. She was one of four boats built in 1921 at the Kirkintilloch canal basin yard of P. McGregor and Sons for a Monmouthshire owner. She was not in southern waters for long and after less than a year was back on the Clyde. Her voyage to the Caledonian Canal will almost certainly have included a passage through the Crinan, so she can probably claim a 'triple crown' of Scottish canals. She was lost in heavy weather off Ardnamurchan in 1952.

93. BEN NEVIS FROM CORPACH.

The Great Glen is part of the most significant geological fault in the British Isles, stretching beyond Caithness in the north and towards Ireland in the south. At the southern end of the glen is the dominating bulk of Britain's highest mountain, Ben Nevis, seen here above the Corpach Locks. The glen and mountains either side are believed to have been formed by the collision of two giant plates of the earth's crust. Granite from Foyers has been matched to rock at Strontian fifty miles away, which also suggests massive lateral movement along the fault line, with the north of Scotland land mass sliding south west.

*Corpach Station and Caledonian Canal.*

At **Corpach** a staircase pair of locks drops the canal from Banavie into the western terminal basin. It is much smaller than Muirtown, but was hacked out of solid rock; a remarkable achievement for the inexperienced navvies. It was reduced in size in the 1960s when the sea lock was extended to allow larger vessels, associated with the pulp mill being built nearby, to use the basin. Although the mill ceased operations in the 1980s, commercial vessels still use the basin. Here, in an earlier age, the basin is occupied by pleasure boats – the large white vessel is a private yacht. Beyond the basin is the single platform Corpach Station on the Mallaig extension of the West Highland Railway.

MacDougall, Fort William      Corpach      Valentines Series

*Saw a diver going down to repair this lock gate.*

The sea lock at Corpach was the first lock on the canal to be finished, although not the first to be started. Work on it could not begin until a huge coffer dam surrounding the construction site was complete and a steam pumping engine installed to keep the workings dry. Once excavation began, work continued uninterrupted until the masonry had been built, the oak gates fitted and the lock made ready to keep out the sea. A wooden pier was built later beside the lock. It allowed steamers to come alongside without having to take time to enter the canal basin. The message under this picture underlines the constant maintenance and vigilance needed to keep this wonderful canal in working order.